The Animal Kingdom

ANIMAL PARTNERSHIPS

Malcolm Penny

Illustrated by Wendy Meadway

The Bookwright Press
New York · 1989

The Animal Kingdom

Animal Adaptations
Animal Camouflage
Animal Defenses
Animal Evolution
Animal Homes
Animal Migration
Animal Movement

Animal Partnerships
Animal Reproduction
Animal Signals
Animals and their Young
Endangered Animals
The Food Chain
Hunting and Stalking

First published in the
United States in 1989 by
The Bookwright Press
387 Park Avenue South
New York, NY 10016

First published in 1988 by
Wayland (Publishers) Ltd
61 Western Road, Hove
East Sussex BN3 1JD, England

Library of Congress Cataloging-in-Publication Data

Penny, Malcolm
   Animal partnerships / Malcolm Penny.
     p. cm. — (The Animal Kingdom)
   Bibliography: p.
   Includes index.
   Summary: Examines the many different ways that plants and animals depend
on each other and help each other survive.
   ISBN 0-531-18223-1
   1. Symbiosis — Juvenile literature.   2. Animal ecology — Juvenile literature.
(1. Symbiosis. 2. Animal ecology.) I. Title. II. Series: Penny, Malcolm.
Animal kingdom.   88–6895
QH548.P46 1989   CIP
591.52′482 — dc19   AC

Typeset by DP Press, Sevenoaks, Kent, England
Printed by Casterman SA, Belgium

All words that appear in **bold** are explained in the glossary on page 30.

Contents

Partners, winners and losers   4

Parasites on the outside   6

Parasites on the inside   8

Partnerships on a coral reef   10

Partners for protection   12

Cleaning services   14

Feeding partners   16

Lookout partnerships   18

Partnerships between animals and plants   20

Ants and their plant partners   22

Ants and their insect partners   24

Cuckoos and cowbirds   26

Partnerships between humans and animals   28

Glossary   30

Further information   30

Index   32

Partners, winners and losers

There are very few animals whose lives are not affected in some way by other animals or by the plants in their **environment**. Sometimes the relationship is rather one-sided, for example between **predators** and the animals they eat. Other partnerships are equal and neither animal is the loser.

The best-balanced partnership is known as **symbiosis**, which means "living together." In this kind of partnership, each animal helps the other.

A good example of a well-balanced partnership is the one that exists between mussels and tiny crabs that live inside mussel shells. The crab picks up food particles that escape from the mussel's filter-feeding

A pea crab living inside a mussel shell. The tiny crab uses its pincers to pick up and feed on small larvae inside the mussel shell. This partnership is useful to both the crab and the mussel.

This large fish, called a coral trout, is not eating the small fish. In fact, it has opened its mouth wide so that the small fish can enter it and carry out a thorough cleaning service, removing specks of food, fungi and parasites that would otherwise harm the coral trout.

system. Neither animal harms the other at all – the crab is safe from its enemies inside the mussel shell, and the mussel benefits because the crab eats the **larvae** of creatures that would harm the mussel if they grew up inside it.

Let us look at another good example of symbiosis. Termites eat wood, but they cannot digest it without the help of **bacteria** that live in their intestines. The bacteria cannot collect wood for themselves, so they benefit from living inside the termites.

Some other animals take what they need for life from another animal, but give nothing back in exchange. Such animals are called parasites. The animal a parasite lives on is called the host.

In this book we shall look at how partnerships work between different animals and some plants. We shall find out which is the winner and which is the loser, or whether both partners are equal.

Parasites on the outside

Parasites often cause or carry serious diseases. All the same, their way of life can be very interesting. External parasites live on the outsides of their hosts, usually feeding on blood. Some of them, like horseflies, leeches or mosquitoes, make only brief visits. Others, such as ticks, fleas and lice, may live their whole lives on the skin of their host.

An external parasite that lives on its host must have some means of hanging on so that it can stay on, even when the host cleans itself. Ticks and lice have strong claws to hang onto an animal's hair. Flatflies, which are parasites of birds, have flat bodies so that they can scuttle very quickly among the feathers. Flatflies and fleas have very tough skins, almost like shells, making them hard to kill.

Illustrated below are a bird louse, a cat flea and a sheep tick. Notice their strong, hooked claws, which they use to cling tightly to the host animal.

Cat flea among cat hairs

Close up

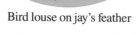

Bird louse on jay's feather

Full size sheep tick swollen with blood

Rabbit fleas, which carry the deadly disease **myxomatosis**, are specially suited to their hosts. When a female rabbit is about to breed, she produces a special chemical in her blood. When the flea sucks up some of this chemical, it too prepares to breed. It does this to make sure that when the new fleas appear, there will be baby rabbits for them to feed on.

Blood-sucking parasites often carry tiny animals inside them, which they pass on to the host animals. These tiny creatures cause diseases that have killed many millions of people, such as malaria and sleeping sickness. That is why the study of parasites is so important to the human race.

The tiny lice that live on huge gray whales are helpful parasites. As the lice feed on the whale's dead skin, they help to loosen troublesome barnacles that grow on the whale's head. After a while the barnacles fall off, helping the whale. In this photograph you can see a tiny louse moving toward some barnacles on the gray whale's mouth.

Parasites on the inside

Almost every animal has one or more **species** of parasite living inside its body. These are called internal parasites. There are so many of them that it is impossible to describe them all in this book. One that is typical is the liver fluke, a type of flat worm that causes sickness among sheep and cattle all over the world.

The liver fluke lives inside the sheep's liver. It produces large numbers of eggs, which land on the grass in the sheep's droppings. The eggs hatch into larvae, which quickly bore their way into the body of a snail. When the larvae have developed to a certain stage, they crawl out of the snail and back onto the grass. When a sheep eats the grass, the liver fluke larvae enter its body. They make their way from its gut into its liver, where they develop into adult flukes and start the cycle again.

The diagram below shows the life cycle of a liver fluke, which is a parasite of sheep and cattle.

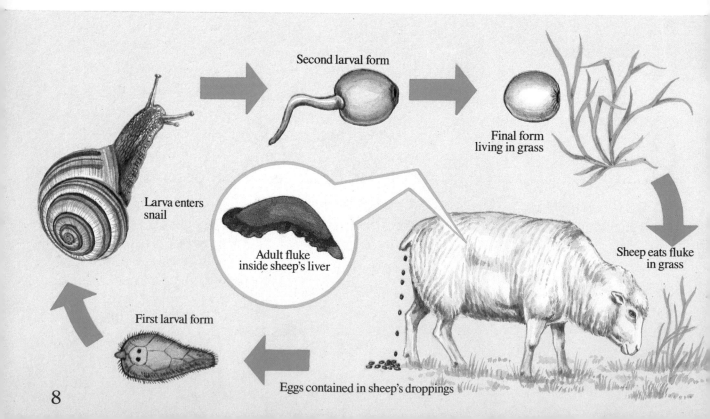

Second larval form

Final form living in grass

Larva enters snail

Adult fluke inside sheep's liver

Sheep eats fluke in grass

First larval form

Eggs contained in sheep's droppings

This pair of flashlight fish of the Indian Ocean have a luminous white stripe beneath each eye. The glowing white light is produced by bacteria that live inside the skin beneath the stripes. The fish can cover the luminous stripes with a shield of black skin, or can uncover them to produce a bright flash of light.

The snail in the life cycle of the liver fluke is called its "secondary host": the fluke's main host is the sheep. Some secondary hosts, such as mosquitoes, are very dangerous because they actually look for victims to bite. When they do so, they pass on the parasites they are carrying. Different species of mosquitoes carry different kinds of **single-celled** parasites, which cause a number of serious diseases, such as malaria and yellow fever.

Some internal parasites are good for their hosts, like the bacteria that live inside termites. A different type of bacteria live inside deep-sea fish and squid. The bacteria gain food and safety from their host. In return they produce light, which helps the fish or squid to find their way around in the deep, dark oceans, and sometimes helps them catch their prey, which are drawn to the light.

Partnerships on a coral reef

The tiny animals that build coral reefs in shallow tropical seas are rather like little sea anemones. They collect chemicals from the sea and use them to make the stony tubes in which they live. When the animals die, others build new tubes on top of those that are left behind, and so the coral reef grows.

Although coral animals find some of their food by filtering specks of food from the sea, they need more than that to survive. They obtain food by means of symbiosis with thousands of tiny single-celled plants, which live inside every coral animal. The plants are called **algae**, and they use sunlight to make food for themselves and oxygen. In fact, they make more food than they need, and the coral uses the leftovers.

Grunts

Angel fish

Cup coral

Parrot fish

Sea squirts

The partnership is not one-sided. The plants gain from it by using the waste products of the coral, especially **carbon dioxide**, to make more food.

Giant clams, which live on coral reefs, also have algae inside their bodies. The giant clam is an enormous shellfish that feeds by filtering the water, but it, too, needs the algae to help it live.

All the filter-feeders that live on the reef help to make life easier for the coral. They keep the water clear, so sunlight can reach the algae and enable them to make their food.

Coral reefs offer shelter to many different kinds of animals, all of which could be said to be the coral's partners in one way or another. The extra oxygen made by the algae inside the coral helps to keep the other animals alive.

The sea creatures of Australian coral reefs all depend on the coral and its partnership with plants.

Brain coral

Saddleback butterfly fish

Copper-banded butterfly fish

Stag's horn coral

Sea slug

Giant clam

Partners for protection

A particular species of crab that lives on coral reefs in the Indian Ocean has a most unusual way of defending itself against its enemies. It picks up a small sea anemone in each claw and waves it at any creature that attacks it. The anemone has stinging cells in its **tentacles**, which can hurt the attacker and drive it away.

Hermit crabs also use anemones as a means of defense. They live on most seashores around the world, and because the crab's own skin is soft and unprotected, it lives inside the shells of dead whelks and other shellfish. When it grows too large, it has to change the shell in which it lives. Every time the hermit crabs needs to change shells, it pushes the new shell close to an anemone growing on a rock.

The crab Lybia tesselata *lives in coral reefs of the Indian Ocean. It carries a stinging anemone in each claw to scare away its enemies.*

A hermit crab living inside an empty whelk shell protected by sea anemones.

The anemone climbs onto the crab's secondhand shell and travels around with it. The anemone **camouflages** the crab and frightens its enemies. At the same time, the anemone benefits from being carried around by the hermit crab to new feeding places, and being able to pick up scraps from the crab's meals. Since both partners do well from this partnership, we could call it symbiosis.

Jellyfish and anemones feed by catching fish with the stinging cells on their tentacles. Two types of fish, called damsel fish and clown fish, find protection from their enemies by living among the tentacles, without being stung themselves. Nobody knows quite how they do it, but it seems as if they become **immune** to the stings of a particular jellyfish or anemone by gently brushing against it.

Other fish find protection by hiding among the spines of sea urchins, where their enemies dare not try to attack them.

A colorful clown fish nestles among the stinging tentacles of an anemone without being stung by them. Here it is quite safe from its enemies, which would be stung as soon as they touched the anemone's tentacles.

13

Cleaning services

A red rock crab, also called the sally lightfoot crab, climbs over a marine iguana, picking off troublesome ticks from the lizard's body. This partnership provides food for the crab and a cleaning service for the iguana.

Large fish on coral reefs share a partnership with little fish called cleaners. They remove and eat parasites and bits of dead skin from large fish. The big fish help them by hanging still in the water, with mouth and gills open so that the cleaners can get inside. You can see a photograph of this on page 5. Cleaner fish are often brightly colored, to make sure that they are not mistaken for food.

On the Galapagos Islands, in the Pacific Ocean, there are large swimming lizards called marine iguanas. They suffer from ticks, which dig into their skin to suck their blood. Red rock crabs climb around on the iguanas' backs, pulling the ticks off and eating them. The iguanas roll over so that the crabs can clean their bellies as well.

In Africa, Egyptian plovers and jacanas, or lily trotters, often hop between the jaws of crocodiles to remove pieces of food and parasites that the crocodile cannot remove for itself. Although crocodiles often eat birds, these birds are never taken.

Another African bird that cleans other animals is the ox-pecker, or tick bird. It removes parasites and damaged skin from large **herbivores**, such as antelope and buffalo. The ox-pecker lives most of its life on the back of its host, even pulling out a few animal hairs to take away to line its nest.

In the northern U.S., the brown-headed cowbird lives in the same way. Before the herds of buffalo were overhunted and disappeared from the prairies, the cowbirds used to follow them. Now they feed on ticks on the cattle that replaced the buffalo.

Opposite *Egyptian plovers can enter the terrifying jaws of the Nile crocodile without being eaten because they provide a cleaning service.*

Feeding partners

Birds and mammals have partnerships that do not necessarily involve one cleaning the other. In Africa and also in North America cattle egrets follow large mammals as they move across the plains. The cattle egret is a small heron that walks in the grass, snapping up insects and other small animals that are disturbed by the movements of the cattle. Sometimes it climbs aboard the cattle to search for ticks, as though it were an ox-pecker.

There is a most remarkable, perfect partnership in Africa between a mammal called the ratel, or honey badger, and a small bird called the honey guide. The ratel eats anything it can find, including plant roots and insects and other small animals. However, it is particularly fond of sweet things, especially honey.

Some cattle egrets feeding among a herd of grazing buffalo in the northern United States.

The honey guide also feeds at bees' nests, but it is not strong enough to break into them. It needs a partner to do this.

When the honey guide finds a bees' nest, it flies off to look for a ratel. It lands in front of it, and hops around, calling and fluttering, until it has attracted the ratel's attention. It then leads the ratel to the bees' nest. Because it loves honey, the ratel at once breaks the nest open. Once the nest is open, the honey guide eats the bees' grubs and the wax inside the nest.

The honey guide will also lead other species of mammal to bees' nests, including people. The Bushmen who live in Botswana, in southern Africa, often follow the birds to find honey; but when they open the nest they always leave the grubs and wax for the bird to eat.

An African honey guide has led a honey badger to a wild bees' nest. The bird will wait for the honey badger to open the nest using its strong claws, and then both animals will feed there.

Lookout partnerships

We have already looked at the partnerships between cattle egrets, ox-peckers, cowbirds and the animals they follow. However, these birds provide another service, besides removing parasites and keeping the host animal's skin clean. If they see a dangerous animal, the birds fly up in alarm, calling so that their host knows that a predator is approaching. Some people have even seen cattle egrets pecking at the head of the animal on which they are riding, as if to tell it to get a move on!

In the jungles of India, the peacock also warns other animals of approaching danger. If it sees a tiger coming, the peacock calls loudly. The other animals know immediately what the call means and watch for the tiger, ready to run for their lives.

There is a strange partnership between two African animals, the baboon and the impala, a kind of antelope. When they are at a water hole, drinking with many other species of animals, baboons and impala usually stay close together. They do this because each can help the other.

The impala is very sharp-eyed and alert for danger because it has so many predators, including lions, cheetahs and leopards. Baboons are not so alert, but they are very fierce, and work as a team to fight their worst enemy, leopards. If the herd of impala smells, hears or sees a predator coming, their nervous behavior warns the baboons as well. They may even attack the enemy and drive it away.

Some impala at a waterhole have sensed that a leopard is nearby and react nervously. This warns the baboons of the danger and one of them shrieks in alarm.

Partnerships between animals and plants

The simplest partnership between animals and plants is that between herbivores and the plants they eat. The plants provide food for the animals, while the animals enrich the soil with their droppings. Animals also help to spread the plants' seeds, either in their droppings or by carrying them on their fur or feathers.

Many flowers can only be **pollinated** by an animal, usually an insect such as a bee, although some flowers are pollinated by birds or even bats. The animals pollinate the flowers as they visit them to collect **nectar** or pollen for food.

By their colors and markings, flowers attract insects to pollinate them. The patterns of lines and spots help to guide the insects into the flower, so that they not only find the nectar but also touch the male and female parts of the flower.

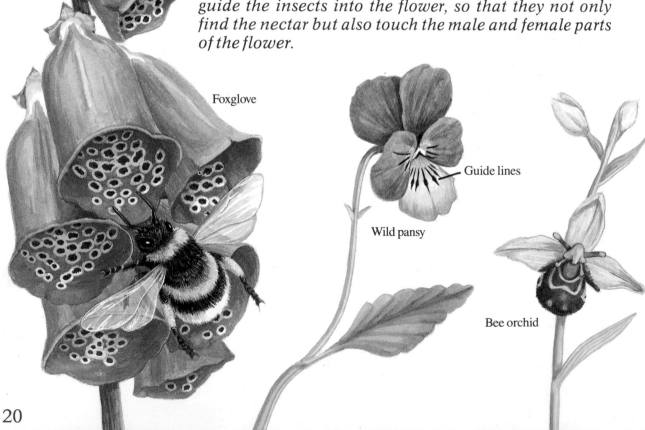

Foxglove

Wild pansy

Guide lines

Bee orchid

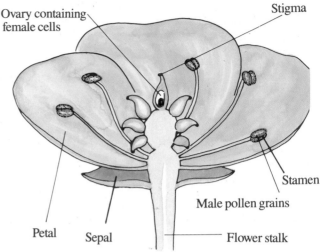

Ovary containing female cells

Stigma

Petal

Sepal

Male pollen grains

Stamen

Flower stalk

Insects can see colors, such as **ultraviolet**, which are invisible to mammals, including humans. Many flowers have ultraviolet guide markings on their petals. These help insects to find the nectar and pollen, which are sometimes found deep inside the flower, and so ensure that the plant will be pollinated.

Some flowers are so specialized that they can only be pollinated by one species of animal. An amazing example is the partnership between a tiny moth and the yucca, a cactus-like plant that grows in the southern United States and Central America.

The female moth collects a ball of pollen from one yucca flower and carries it to another. Before she pollinates the new flower, she lays some eggs inside the flower's **ovary**, where the seeds will be produced. When her caterpillars hatch, they eat some of the seeds before lowering themselves to the ground, where they **pupate** and wait for next spring. They leave most of the seeds in the plant, to grow into new plants in the next season.

No other animal can pollinate the yucca plant, and the caterpillar has no other food: neither of these partners could live without the other.

Above left *A tiny yucca moth pollinates a yucca flower. This very special partnership is an example of how two species depend on each other totally for survival.*

Above right *This cutaway diagram of a buttercup flower shows its male and female parts. An insect or bird visiting the flower to collect nectar will brush against the male stamens and take pollen grains to the female stigma. The flower must be fertilized before it can produce seed.*

Ants and their plant partners

Some species of ants, especially those that live in South and Central America, are expert farmers. There are two main kinds, leaf-cutter ants and bromeliad ants, both of which have a partnership with plants.

Leaf-cutter ants collect leaves from trees, and take the cut-up pieces into a huge underground chamber they have dug out. There they chew up the leaves, moistening them with their own **saliva**. Next they plant the tiny **spores** of a fungus on the chewed-up leaves. When the fungus grows, the ants collect it to use as food for themselves and their young. When the ants move on, they take some of the spores with them to start a new fungus garden.

Brazilian leaf-cutter ants carry pieces of leaves to make their nest.

Bromeliad ants are even more extraordinary. They live inside bromeliads, plants like pineapples that grow in the Amazon jungle. Because the Amazon region is often flooded, the ground is not safe for either plants or animals, which might get washed away or drowned.

The ants avoid this problem by carrying the seeds of the bromeliad up into the branches of a tree, and planting them in little patches of mud, which they have already carried up there for that purpose. The plant develops roots, which wrap around the branch, high above the danger of floods at ground level. Its stems and leaves provide the ants with a safe place for their nest. Being up in the tree not only makes the bromeliad safer, it also enables the plant to find more sunshine, and so grow better, away from the shady forest floor.

A bromeliad ant (left foreground) carries a bromeliad seed into the branch of a tree, where it will plant the seed. Other bromeliad plants are growing on the branch, safely above the flooded ground in the Amazon jungle of South America.

Ants and their insect partners

Some species of ants live in partnership with other insects. The best known are those ants that "farm" aphids. As they feed, the aphids produce a sweet-tasting substance called honeydew, which the ants like to eat. By stroking them with their **antennae**, the ants encourage the aphids to produce the honeydew. The aphids gain from the partnership because the ants protect them against beetles and other predators.

Some butterflies have caterpillars that can produce honeydew. The imperial blue butterfly lives in Australia. It lays its eggs in ants' nests, and its caterpillar is looked after by ants from the moment it hatches.

When the caterpillar pupates, the ants still guard it, but when it emerges as an adult butterfly, it no longer produces honeydew. This causes the ants to change their behavior, and they will eat the butterfly unless it flies away very quickly. Because of this, the imperial blue must be able to fly as soon as it emerges from its pupa.

The large blue butterfly in Europe is also brought up by ants in exchange for honeydew. The caterpillar is "kidnapped" by a red ant, which takes it into its underground nest, where all the other ants protect it. They even feed the caterpillar with their own grubs to encourage it to produce the delicious liquid. When the butterfly emerges, it walks out of the ants' nest, only expanding its wings when it is clear of the tunnels and can fly away.

A black ant feeds on a delicious drop of honeydew, which it has "milked" from an aphid.

Opposite *Two red ants are carrying a large blue larva to their nest, where they will look after it until it emerges as a butterfly. In the background two newly-emerged large blue butterflies rest on a thyme plant, where the female will lay her eggs.*

Cuckoos and cowbirds

Cuckoos are called "nest parasites," because they lay their eggs, and leave their young to be fed and reared in other birds' nests. When the European cuckoo hatches, it throws the eggs and young of its **foster parents** out of the nest, so that it is the only bird to be fed by the parents.

A female cuckoo lays her eggs in the nest of the same species of bird that fed her when she was a baby. The egg looks very similar to the bird's own eggs, and the parents accept it and look after it, even though it is much bigger than one of their own. When the chick hatches, the foster parents feed it, even though it grows bigger than them. They are the losers in this partnership, because they are prevented from rearing any young of their own for the season.

A full-grown dunnock, or hedge sparrow, feeds a grub to a cuckoo chick, which is already much larger than its foster parent, the dunnock.

Cowbirds are also nest parasites, but their hosts are not always complete losers. In Central America, cowbirds are parasites in the nests of a small bird called the oropendola. The cowbird chicks do not throw out the oropendola chicks, but help them to survive.

Oropendola chicks suffer from a parasite called a botfly, whose larvae burrow into their bodies and often kill them. Young cowbirds usefully remove the larvae from their foster brothers and sisters.

Cowbirds need to be nest parasites because their old habit of following the herds of American bison did not give them time to stop to build nests and rear chicks of their own. Instead, they **evolved** a way of making sure that other birds would hatch and look after their chicks for them.

Inside the ball-shaped nest of the oropendola, a cowbird chick removes parasites from the oropendola chick. Although the cowbird chick is a parasite, it provides a useful service and helps the oropendola chick to survive.

27

Partnerships between humans and animals

There are many important partnerships between humans and animals. In the countryside they are easy to see. People keep cattle in order to have milk, meat, and leather; they rear chickens for eggs and meat, and sheep for meat and wool. In some countries, cattle are used to help plow the land. In countries like Britain, Australia and New Zealand, some breeds of dogs are the farmer's partners in rounding up the sheep.

In the town, the partnerships are not so obvious, but they are still important. Dogs guard buildings or help the police and guide blind people around the streets. Horses provide exercise for riders and entertainment for spectators in racing, show-jumping, and in big parades.

Animals can form a good working partnership with people. In the picture a team of ponies and cattle work together threshing rice in Northern Pakistan.

Cats do more than look beautiful and keep mice away: they provide company for people, and even help to keep them well. Sitting quietly stroking a purring cat is a very good way to relax, and it can help prevent stress.

Many animals choose to live close to humans. Some of the partnerships are very one-sided, such as those between humans and mice, carpet beetles or clothes moths, which are all a nuisance and could be called parasites. Some wild animals are useful partners for humans. In Europe hedgehogs and thrushes eat garden pests, such as slugs and snails, while in the United States and Canada rat snakes eat rats and mice in farm buildings.

We have looked at many kinds of partnerships, both useful and harmful. All animals are partners in one way, because we are all part of the richness and beauty of the animal kingdom.

Many people share a special partnership with their pets. Of course, a pet benefits by being fed and looked after, but it usually enjoys and returns the friendship and affection of its owner.

Glossary

Algae (singular **alga**) Very simple plants that usually consist of one cell and grow in water.

Antennae (singular **antenna**) The pair of "feelers" on an insect's head.

Bacteria Organisms that consist of one cell.

Camouflages Conceals or hides.

Carbon dioxide A colorless, odorless gas that plants use to make food.

Environment An animal's surroundings including the soil, air, water, plants and other animals.

Evolved Developed or changed to suit a particular purpose.

Foster parents Parents who look after someone else's young for a time.

Herbivores Animals that eat only plants.

Immune No longer affected by a disease or a substance, having gradually become used to it.

Larvae (singular **larva**) The young form of insects that have hatched from eggs.

Myxomatosis A disease that affects, and often kills, rabbits.

Nectar A sugary fluid produced by flowers to attract insects and birds to pollinate them.

Ovary The female part of a flower that produces ovules, which become seeds.

Pollinate To carry pollen to the stigma of a flower.

Predators Animals that live by eating other animals, which are called **prey.**

Pupate To change from a caterpillar into a cocoon.

Saliva The colorless liquid produced in the mouth to help digest food.

Single-celled Consisting of one cell.

Species A group of animals or plants that is different from all other groups.

Spores Reproductive cells released by fungi.

Symbiosis A close partnership between two animal or plant species that depend on each other for survival.

Tentacles The arms of an octopus, squid or sea anemone.

Ultraviolet Light that exists beyond the violet end of the color spectrum visible to humans. Unlike humans, insects are able to see this light.

Further information

To find out more about animal partnerships, you might like to read the titles below:

Animal Cooperation: A Look at Sociobiology by Hallie Black. William Morrow, 1981.

Animals That Live in Groups by Gwynne Vevers. Merrimack Publishers Circulation, Distributed by Associated Booksellers, 1981.

Discovering Ants by Christopher O'Toole. The Bookwright Press, 1988.

How Animals Live by Philip Steele. Franklin Watts, 1985.

How Animals Live Together by Millicent E. Selsam. William Morrow, 1979.

There are some excellent wildlife films shown on television that may include examples of animals that live in partnership. Look in particular for films about coral reefs and the African grasslands.

If you would like to learn more about wild animals, and help to protect them, you might like to join one of the organizations listed below:

Audubon Naturalist Society
of the Central Atlantic States
8940 Jones Mill Road
Chevy Chase, Maryland 20815

The Conservation Foundation
1717 Massachusetts Avenue, N.W.
Washington, D.C. 20036

Greenpeace
1611 Connecticut Avenue, N.W.
Washington, D.C. 20009

The Humane Society of the USA
2100 L Street, N.W.
Washington, D.C. 20037

The International Fund
for Animal Welfare
P.O. Box 193
Yarmouth Port, Massachusetts 02675

National Wildlife Federation
1412 16th Street, N.W.
Washington, D.C. 20036

The World Wildlife Fund
1255 23d Street, N.W.
Washington, D.C. 20037

Picture acknowledgments

The publishers would like to thank the following for allowing their photographs to be reproduced in this book: Bruce Coleman Limited 4 (Jane Burton), 5 (Bill Wood), 14 (David Houston), 21 (M Fogden); Oxford Scientific Films 13 (David Shall); Seaphot 9 (Ken Lucas); Survival Anglia 7 (Jeff Foott); ZEFA 22 (R Halin), 29 (Schaefer). The illustration on page 21 is by Cecilia Fitzsimons.

Index

Africa 14, 16, 17, 19
Algae 10, 11
Antelope 14
    impala 19
Ants 22, 23, 24
    bromeliad 22, 23
    leaf-cutter 22
    red 24
Aphids 24
Australia 10, 24, 28

Baboons 19
Bacteria 5, 9
Bees 17, 20
Birds 6, 14, 16, 17, 18, 24
Botflies 27
Britain 28
Bromeliads 23
Buffalo 14, 27
Bushmen 17
Butterflies 24
    imperial blue 24
    large blue 24

Canada 29
Cats 29
Caterpillars 21, 24
Cattle 14, 28
Cattle egrets 14, 18
Central America 21, 26
Chickens 26, 27, 28
Clams, giant 11
Cleaning 14, 16
Corals 10, 11, 12
Coral reefs 10, 11, 14
Cowbirds 14, 18, 26, 27
Crabs 4, 5, 12, 14
    hermit 12, 13
    pea 4
    red rock 14

Crocodiles 14
Cuckoos 26

Diseases 6, 7, 9
Dogs 28

Egg-laying 21, 24
Europe 24, 29

Feeding partners 16–17
Fish 9, 13, 14
    cleaner 5, 14
    clown 13
    damsel 13
Flatflies 6
Fleas 6, 7
Flowers 20, 21
Fungi 22

Galapagos Islands 14

Hedgehogs 29
Honeydew 24
Honey guides 16, 17
Horseflies 6
Host animals 5, 6, 9, 14,
    18, 27
Humans 7, 21, 28

Iguanas, marine 14
India 18

Jacanas 14
Jellyfish 13

Leeches 6
Leopards 19
Lice 6
Liver flukes 8, 9
Look-out partners 18–19

Mice 29
Mosquitoes 6, 9
Moths 21
    yucca 21
    clothes 29
Mussels 4, 5
Myxomatosis 7

New Zealand 28

Oropendolas 27
Ox-peckers 14, 16, 18

Parasites 5, 6, 7, 8, 9, 14,
    18, 29
    internal 8, 9
    external 6, 7
    nest 26, 27
Pets 29
Plants 5, 10, 11, 16, 20, 21,
    22, 23
Plovers, Egyptian 14
Pollination 20, 21
Protection partnerships
    12–13

Rabbits 7
Ratels 16, 17

Sea anemones 10, 12, 13
Sea urchins 13
Seeds 20, 21, 22
Snakes, rat 29
South America 22
Symbiosis 4, 5, 10, 13

Termites 5, 9
Ticks 6, 14, 16

United States 14, 29